A Childre

Picture Books: The Write W
A Children's Writer Insider (

MW01297056

written by Lisa Bullard and Laura Purdie Salas

A Note from the Mentors:
At many points in our careers as working writers, we've benefitted
from the advice of other writers who have "been there, done that"
before us. As Mentors for Rent, we're delighted to in turn be able to
pass along some of the information we've learned through our
personal experiences and observations of writers we know and
admire. We hope that you find the advice we share useful as you
consider the next steps in pursuing your writing dreams. But we
certainly don't intend that you take what we have to say as a
replacement for legal or financial expertise. As we remind you in
this guide, it's always critical that you do thorough research and then
make your decisions based on your own judgment of what's best for
you and your career.

And this is a gentle reminder that when we call ourselves "working
writers," we really mean it. Our writing has made us rich in
experience and personal satisfaction, but nowhere remotely close to
rich in regards to our bankbooks! We've kept this guide as
affordable as possible in the hopes that you'll recommend that your
friends buy their own copy, rather than redistributing your copy to
them.

First Edition - 2013
Cover based on a design by Ranilo Cabo

1

Mentors for Rent

Balanced advice about writing and publishing

MentorsForRent.com

Picture Books the Write Way

Picture Books: The Write Way

PICTURE BOOKS: THE WRITE WAY....................**5**

INTRODUCTION: STRENGTHEN YOUR PICTURE BOOK MANUSCRIPT BY ASKING 10 KEY QUESTIONS..**7**

QUESTION 1: IS IT A SHORT STORY INSTEAD? 11

QUESTION 2: DOES IT LACK A FRESH TAKE?....**15**

QUESTION 3: IS IT TOO LONG? **17**

QUESTION 4: IS IT UNFOCUSED? **19**

QUESTION 5: WILL YOUNG KIDS FAIL TO RELATE?..**21**

QUESTION 6: IS IT TOO NOSTALGIC? **23**

QUESTION 7: IS THE POINT OF VIEW INEFFECTIVE?..**25**

QUESTION 8: IS IT TOO QUIET?......................**27**

QUESTION 9: ARE THERE ILLUSTRATION ISSUES? **31**

QUESTION 10: IS YOUR METER IMPERFECT?....**33**

REVISION CHECKLIST **37**

TELL US HOW IT GOES FOR YOU! **39**

INTRODUCTION: STRENGTHEN YOUR PICTURE BOOK MANUSCRIPT BY ASKING 10 KEY QUESTIONS

Our goal as Mentors for Rent is to share what we've learned during our many years as published children's book writers and writing teachers—to provide advice that helps other writers avoid the mistakes we've made and benefit from the shortcuts we've discovered.

Picture books are especially close to both our hearts. We've been fortunate enough to work with fantastic editors on the way to having our own published. And over the years, we've coached hundreds of other picture book writers, offering them feedback about how they can make their manuscripts stronger and more marketable in today's competitive publishing environment.

There are 10 key concerns that we end up addressing over and over again when we do picture book critiques. Many manuscripts we see have 2 or 3 of these problems in place—and almost every manuscript we critique has at least 1 of them! So we decided to focus on those 10 issues in this series of short essays. Each essay highlights one of the 10 key questions you will want to ask yourself about your manuscript. And if you find that your answer is "Yes—that is a problem for me," we offer easy-to-apply writing tips to help you address that concern in your revisions.

Some of the advice we give here applies primarily to narrative picture books (those that tell a story), because that's the type of picture book we are most often asked to critique. But a lot of what we offer also applies to other types of picture books. Before you dig further, we want to outline some basics about the kind of narrative picture books being published in the current marketplace:

- In a true picture book, the illustrations tell half the story. But choosing the illustrator is not up to you as the writer.

- Picture books (with the exception of some nonfiction titles) need to be relatable for a pre-reading audience (think in terms of a small child snuggled on a lap as an adult reads). If you're picturing older readers, your story is probably not best suited for a picture book.

- Very short picture books are the current norm; editors are pushing for manuscripts under 500 words and absolutely under 1,000 words (nonfiction is sometimes an exception).

- There should be some conflict/tension in your story, even if it's only the kind of obstacle a small child would face (having to take a nap, for example). Humorous conflict sells really well in the current marketplace.

- Rhyme is not necessary, and in fact many editors claim they dislike rhyming verse. If you have written in rhyme, editors will often encourage you to try the story without the rhyme.

We also encourage you to go to the library or bookstore and read loads of brand-new picture books—not the nostalgic favorites from yesteryear, but those that have come out in the past few months—so that you will really start to grasp what current editors are looking for.

Then, for those of you who are complete newcomers to the picture book format, we encourage you to tackle each of the topics we present here at your own pace. Try applying each one to your writing as you go through the guide.

For those of you who've been writing picture books a little longer, use the guide as a handy revision checklist. You can work through it in the order we present it, or you can read down the Table of Contents and start by tackling a pitfall you recognize from your own writing. Whatever order you read through them, the essays will all give you guidance on how you can write a more marketable manuscript.

And for those of you who have gotten as far as submitting your work, but haven't yet seen success, this guide is a way to work towards identifying the things that might be holding you back from making a publishing match.

We've given you 10 possible ways to strengthen your picture book manuscript and turn it into something that is more likely to catch an editor's eye—so dig in and learn how to create a picture book the "write" way!

Picture Books the Write Way

QUESTION 1: IS IT A SHORT STORY INSTEAD?

For several years, I submitted what I thought were picture books to editors. None of them sold as picture books. Later, though, several of them sold as short stories. Now I recognize how telling that was.

A true picture book manuscript would very rarely work as a short story, or vice versa. What I had were short story manuscripts, not picture book manuscripts.

Now I think of a picture book text like one beautiful fall maple leaf, able to represent an entire season or mood through its spareness. But a short story is like the entire maple tree, full of details and variety and a feeling of completion.

For instance, here's the opening to a picture book manuscript about a giraffe I worked on a while back:

McCall was too tall. There's no other way to say it. It caused problems everywhere he went.
One week was the most terrible week of all.

Monday night, he went with his friend Zookie to the movies. [illo note: Zookie is NOT a giraffe.] The lady behind them told McCall to take off his ridiculous hat. But he wasn't wearing a hat—that was his neck!

Tuesday, McCall flew to visit Grandma…

And here's the same opening, cast as a short story manuscript:

McCall the giraffe was too tall. Everywhere he went, his long, long neck got in the way. He did the best he could not to cause problems…until the very worst week of all.

On Monday, he went with his friend Zookie the hedgehog to see the new Supersheep movie. The lady sitting behind them said, "Take off that ridiculous hat! I can't see a thing!"

McCall sighed and slumped in his chair. He wasn't wearing a hat! But his long neck was blocking the screen.

Tuesday, McCall flew in a real airplane to visit his grandma...

Can you hear the difference? Here are some ways picture books and short stories are different:

• A picture book must have enough visual possibilities for at least 13 different illustrations. If your text would work in a children's magazine such as **Ladybug** or **Highlights** with one or two fantastic illustrations, then you have a short story. Making a book-dummy can help you distinguish which one you have. There's a helpful post from Tara Lazar at http://tinyurl.com/q8acpej if you need help creating a dummy.

• A picture book often covers more ground--even weeks or months in a character's life. A short story, on the other hand, often has one scene covering a very short time.

• A picture book must resonate. Editor Allyn Johnston of Beach Lane Books compares picture books to miniature pieces of theater. They strike a chord with kids and demand re-reading. With short stories, though, one reading is usually enough.

• A picture book is meant to be read aloud. It has rhythm, and the sound of the words is extremely important. A short story is about the story, while a picture book is about the entire read-aloud experience.

• A picture book doesn't have much descriptive detail. In fact, without the art, the text often sounds too bare bones. That's because a picture book is a true collaboration, and the art supplies half the story.

•   A picture book might have dialog, but it only hints at the full conversation. It's not as complete as the dialog in a short story.

There are exceptions, of course. But if you read many, many recently published picture books, you'll start to absorb the feel of what contemporary editors are looking for.

In fact, start right now. Get 20 recently published picture books and 10 issues of children's magazines that target 4-8 year olds. Read all the books and stories. Read them aloud. Even better, record yourself reading your favorites. Wait a few days and listen back to them.

The listening part is important! In picture books, the gaps left for the illustrator to fill in will be more obvious that way. Now read aloud your own manuscript. Record it. Listen back. What do you hear? A picture book or a short story?

If it's a picture book, great! If it sounds like a short story, then it's time to decide whether you want to 1) revise it with a goal of turning it into a picture book or 2) revise it with an eye to submitting it to magazine markets.

Picture books are not inherently better than short stories. They are two different genres, and correctly identifying what you're writing will help you in your marketing/publishing efforts!

--Laura Purdie Salas

Picture Books the Write Way

QUESTION 2: DOES IT LACK A FRESH TAKE?

Baseball great Yogi Berra is credited with coining the expression "déjà vu all over again." There was a great example of this in 2012, when 2 picture books, published within 7 months of each other, shared the same description, even down to many details: "a humorous alphabet story that features an unruly animal who refuses to stick with his own page of the alphabet, while a Zebra tries to restore order."

In this case, it's likely that nobody involved with the books even knew the other existed until both were well on the way to being published, because illustrated books take a long time to produce. And both books went on to be well-received by reviewers. But I imagine that the creators couldn't help asking themselves, "Will readers really buy 2 titles that seem so similar? Or will they choose one over the other?" I leave it to you to compare *Z Is for Moose* (written by Kelly Bingham) and *A Is for Musk Ox* (written by Erin Cabatingan) to see for yourself whether you'd purchase both titles.

A similar coincidence has come to light many times during my years as a writing teacher / mentor; it seems true, in fact, that there are only a limited number of good story ideas. A panicked picture book writer will approach me having just discovered that the manuscript he or she has poured love and energy into is "just like" a book that has already been published. There are a couple of important lessons here that can help you avoid just such a moment: first, read widely (immerse yourself in dozens and dozens of newly published picture books a year). And remember how important it is to research your story concepts to see if there are already-published titles that might be direct competition.

But if you discover that your story idea is not completely original—which is all-too-often the case—are you out of luck? Not necessarily. The trick is to make sure you are approaching the concept in a way that feels fresh and original.

Again, study the competition. Do many titles seem to share the same basic story? Then make sure you have pushed yourself to find a very different angle or approach to this same core story. Could you tell the story from a different point of view? With a surprising twist at the end? Set in an unexpected setting? Representing a different cultural perspective? Brainstorm a long list of ways that you could make your approach stand out from its competitors while still retaining the same core story or idea.

Here are a couple of examples. Looking to convey the idea that "the earth gives us everything we need," Doreen Cronin takes a fresh approach to this common environmental theme. She does so by delivering her message through an unexpected perspective: the hilarious diary entries of a young earthworm (*Diary of a Worm*).

Want to tell a story about the risks of bringing home a wild animal as a pet? Why not go for a fresh take by reversing the roles and having a young bear bring home a human child (all with vastly humorous consequences)? That's how Peter Brown gave this familiar childhood impulse a fresh spin in *Children Make Terrible Pets*.

There may be no new stories under the sun, but you can push yourself to find a fresh new way to tell the same old story!

--Lisa Bullard

QUESTION 3: IS IT TOO LONG?

One challenging reality is that picture books—which have always been short—are trending even shorter. Publishers say they'd prefer to see writers come in at 500 or fewer words; 800 or so words seems to be the maximum for most stories. Every time I read my picture book *Trick-or-Treat on Milton Street* to kids (it weighs in at a bit over 800 words), I edit the text as I go, because I've learned by reading out loud where I should have made cuts in the first place! That means you're going to need to cut your 1,500-word manuscript—the one you can't imagine cutting by even one word—in half! So what are some of the tactics you can use?

Make sure everything points back to one central focus. We go into more detail about this in another section. The thing to remember when you're cutting is that everything in a picture book must relate to the core of the book. Cut any scenes, characters, settings, or words that don't point back to that focus.

Get rid of extra characters. Ask yourself if every character in the story is absolutely necessary (especially the adult characters). Who could you get rid of without truly affecting the story?

Look to see if any story sections are too text-heavy. Print off your manuscript. Draw brackets around each section of text that you imagine accompanying one illustration. Examples of where you'd put a new set of brackets include: the character changes location, someone new enters the story, the character discovers new information, the character makes a new attempt to solve her problem. Look at each text block. Is one much longer? That's a place to start cutting first.

Don't do the illustrator's job. Unless they're necessary to the understanding of the story, leave most visual details to the illustrator.

For example: if the fact that Abby has freckles matters, tell us about them. But if it doesn't really matter what Abby looks like (or even whether she's a human little girl or a little bear), then cut the description and let the illustrator decide.

Highlight every verb. Is each one as strong as possible? Or have you used a weaker verb paired with an adverb? Switch to one strong verb, and you've cut your word use. Here's an example: instead of saying "Caleb ran quickly," say "Caleb dashed" or "Caleb raced." The substitutions are more descriptive and use fewer words.

Challenge every adjective. Sometimes a list of several adjectives actually buries the reader in too much detail. Instead, choose the most telling adjective and cut the rest. The one you do choose will stand out even more.

You may be thinking that it still seems impossible to tell a layered, effective story using fewer than 500 words. But consider a book like **Chalk**, by Bill Thomson, that tells a complete story despite being a wordless picture book. Studying wordless picture books can help you see how much of a picture book is carried by the illustrations. The illustrator will bring much to the story that you don't need to say in actual words. Trust him or her to do a good job!

Or check out **City Dog, Country Frog**, written by Mo Willems. It tells a story using 333 words that even very young children can understand, yet also packs such an emotional punch that adults shed tears when they read it for the first time.

It is possible to write a powerful story in a very few words—and the hard work you put into revising and cutting will help make your picture book manuscript more marketable!

--Lisa Bullard

QUESTION 4: IS IT UNFOCUSED?

Picture books must be tightly focused. They revolve around one very contained core idea, question, or problem. But in many of the picture book drafts that we critique, the writer has included multiple cores—sometimes without being aware of it!

The picture book audience is quite young. The audience members are still listeners rather than readers, and they're still learning how to decode stories. You want to give them one focused through-line that guides them from the beginning to the end of your work. Too many different story cores will confuse or distract them from successfully completing this story journey.

One good test is to ask yourself if the "answer" that is given in the resolution of your story directly answers the "question" that you posed at the beginning. If the question and the answer don't match up, your piece will feel as if there are 2 different stories fighting each other for supremacy. After having this pointed out, some writers recognize that one of their story cores (either the beginning question, or the ending answer that fits a different question) is the one they intended. Other times, the writer sees that both stories have appeal, and after splitting them apart, ends up with 2 stories!

Here's an example from my own experience—a case where I had 2 different story possibilities fighting it out in one manuscript. It took a smart editor to point out to me that in the early draft for my picture book *Not Enough Beds!*, most of the story was sweet, nostalgic, and focused on a quiet grandparent visit. But the beginning of the story hinted at quite a different story: it had a zany rather than sweet tone, it was in rhyme (the rest of the manuscript wasn't), and it allowed for the possibility of an over-the-top family gathering for Christmas with tons of noisy relatives. The editor encouraged me to rewrite the whole story using the beginning premise, and that noisy, zany version has gone on to sell many thousands of copies!

At times there are more than 2 story cores competing for attention. So another good test is to force yourself to summarize the story in one sentence. If you find this very challenging, it may be a sign that there are too many cores competing for the reader's attention. Once you've come up with your one sentence, then it's a good revision tactic to go through every line of the story—every word, even—and challenge it: does it point directly back to that one-sentence story core? If not, then it likely should be deleted.

David LaRochelle's ***The Best Pet of All*** is a fun example. The question at the beginning is: will the character get the dog he so badly wants? At one point the character has an apparent change of heart. But if you carefully study the ending illustrations, you will see that the change of heart is actually part of the character's clever plan to get a dog; the through-line never truly wavers. And the story is easily summarized in one sentence: "A boy brings home a dragon to convince his mother that a dog would make a better pet."

Identify your story's core at the beginning, and then guide the reader to a conclusion that echoes back that same sure note—without being tempted to switch to a different song altogether!

--Lisa Bullard

QUESTION 5: WILL YOUNG KIDS FAIL TO RELATE?

A super common issue is picture book manuscripts that the PBA (picture book audience) can't relate to. Yes, some picture books target older kids of 6 to 8. But those are fairly rare (and many are by big-name authors). An audience of 2 to 5 years old is the sweet spot.

So, consider your story problem. If a kindergartner wouldn't care about it, your manuscript will be a tough sell to a publisher.

Here are some of my own epic-fail picture book ideas.

• A kid is scared about sleepover camp: [Day camp makes more sense.]

• Life in different U.S. regions—What's different and the same about food/houses, etc. [The PBA doesn't care. The PBA cares about its own homes. And maybe the Tooth Fairy's house.]

• Girl is at the pool when her underwear falls out of her pool bag and is humiliated when the lifeguard holds them up for lost and found. [Yes, this is autobiographical. And an 8-year-old would die of embarrassment, but this doesn't work for a 4-year-old.]

I've read picture book manuscripts about preschoolers worrying over a parents' divorce, wondering if Mom will get a new job, and discussing taxes in classroom elections. These are adult concerns, for the most part. They do impact preschoolers' lives, but internal problems and complex issues don't generally make for good picture books. Things (that can be illustrated!) need to happen in picture books. Any topic/conflict that requires explanation weighs down your manuscript.

Here are some picture books I've loved recently, along with each one's PBA-friendly core problem:

- ***The Sniffles for Bear***, by Bonny Becker – Bear thinks his friend Mouse does NOT appreciate how sick Bear is. What preschooler has not felt that way?

- ***I Must Have Bobo!***, by Eileen Rosenthal – Willy's cat Earl keeps stealing Willy's favorite toy. The PBA gets mighty tired of sharing its toys!

- ***Where's Walrus?***, by Stephen Savage – Walrus escapes the zoo. Every preschooler wants to escape grown-ups' schedules!

- ***Me...Jane***, by Patrick McDonnell – Young Jane Goodall dreams of studying animals. This book validates kids' big dreams.

- ***This Is Not My Hat***, by Jon Klassen – A little fish steals a big fish's hat but is sure he can get away with it. OK, the PBA is full of thieves. They just call it "borrowing," since they are not fools.

So, what do you do if you have an idea you want to share in picture book form, but it's NOT easily relatable to the PBA?

1) Condense it enormously and focus on the sparest way to tell that tale. ***Eight Days Gone***, by Linda McReynolds, is a great example of this.

2) Create a way to connect it to your PBA. Mara Rockliff took the topics of the Great Depression and philanthropy and wrote a story with kids as heroes in ***My Heart Will Not Sit Down***.

3) Let go of the idea that it *has* to be a picture book. 99% of the time, if your idea is not inherently appealing to the PBA, you can't force it into picture book form. Lisa has had students who have sold their "picture book" manuscripts to magazines (make nice publishing credits for your picture book cover letter)! Or maybe this idea needs to be a chapter book or a novel. You don't have to abandon it completely. But focus your picture book energy on ideas that are truly picture-book appropriate.

--Laura Purdie Salas

QUESTION 6: IS IT TOO NOSTALGIC?

Everybody loves to hear about the good old days, right?

Wrong.

The kids listening to your book live busy lives of siblings, errand-running, and blankie-gnawing. They do not know about the good old days. They do not care about the good old days.

That might sound a little harsh. But if you're hoping to publish your picture book with a mainstream publisher, nostalgic stories are not the way to go.

Here are 5 signs that your picture book manuscript is nostalgic:

•   The narrator is an adult telling a story from his or her childhood. Flashbacks do not work in picture books. Example: "When I was just 6 years old, something happened that changed my life forever."

•   There's no conflict in your story. People writing with a sense of nostalgia often are reluctant to introduce problems, conflict, drama—all the things that picture books thrive on! Example: "Billy closed his eyes and fell asleep at the close of another perfect day."

•   It is set in some indeterminate time in the past, but it's not a fairy tale. Usually, the language and the obvious omission of modern technology are signs of this. Example: "Mama had packed bread and cheese in my lunch bucket." "Daddy got up from the couch and changed the channel on the television." [Note: This is different from historical fiction picture books, which are pretty rare themselves.]

•   A grown-up is the focus of your story. Many nostalgic writers can't resist making the adult the problem-solver. They are telling the story through adult eyes rather than childlike ones, even if the narrator is a child. Example: "I knew with Mom's help, I would get it right!"

• An idyllic tone accompanies the entire piece. Looking at the world through rose-tinted glasses is what makes any story, even a contemporary one, feel nostalgic. When you create a pastoral, perfect world, infused with old-fashioned values, you can quickly slide into a nostalgic tone. Example: "Sunlight sprinkled down on the lawn as I got out my bicycle."

Nostalgia is a tone that pervades an entire manuscript, so obviously the above examples are limited. One pastoral sentence does not a nostalgic picture book make. So make sure you're reading tons of picture books published within the past couple of years to get a sense for where the line is drawn between a manuscript that depicts a happy, childlike world, and a manuscript that depicts a nostalgic, good-old-days world.

If you want to share your memories of the good old days and stories of your childhood with your own family and friends, that's great. Do it! But know that those stories rarely translate into a salable picture book manuscript. Instead, your stories about simpler times and happier days are memoir pieces and are best shared with other adults rather than with kids.

Kids these days. They just don't care about the good old days.

--Laura Purdie Salas

QUESTION 7: IS THE POINT OF VIEW INEFFECTIVE?

One key to creating a successful picture book is to find a way to put young listeners "inside" the book's experience. Achieving this insider effect can be as simple as choosing a child for the point of view (POV) character. Young listeners will easily bond with another child; this character will become their entry point into the story.

But many picture book writers find themselves relating more to an adult character in the story—and so make the mistake of telling the story from that adult's point of view. So instead of the grandchild's story, it becomes Grandma's story. It's fine to have Grandma IN your story—but don't make the mistake of assuming a small child will find it as easy to identify with Grandma as you do. If an adult is your POV character, ask yourself: Could I somehow retell the same story through a child's eyes?

Sometimes writers choose an adult character because they want children to learn an important message about life through the eyes of an older and wiser adult. Beware if this is your rationale; these stories often come off as heavy-handed and "preachy." It's fine if a message emerges subtly through the action and consequences of the story, but your picture book should never feel moralistic.

Other times, writers choose an older character because it isn't realistic to assume a child would have the kind of freedom the story's plot needs (we're not likely to believe that "One day, 4-year-old Susie was wandering alone through the big woods…"). In that case, you might use an animal character (or as they're sometimes referred to in children's publishing, "kids with fur"). But even these characters need to have an aspect that is recognizable to a human child. Curious George, for example, is as mischievous, curious, and naughty as any human child. Even the Little Engine that Could—a machine!—is a LITTLE engine in a world of larger engines; children connect with the story because the Little Engine, despite his small size, manages to succeed where the big engines don't. Beating out the adults is every small child's dream!

Another thing I've seen go wrong is when a writer chooses an unusual point of view character, such as an inanimate object, but then fails to build a bridge between that character and their young listener. Almost anything could be turned into a child-relatable character, but you do have to build that bridge by giving your unusual character the kind of conflicts that a small child can connect with. For example, in **Chopsticks**, author Amy Krouse Rosenthal manages to make a pair of chopsticks child-friendly by turning them into best friends who are faced with an unexpected hurdle to their relationship. Children root for these non-human characters because they recognize the same bonds of friendship and the anxiety of separation that they have experienced themselves. If instead, the chopsticks in the story were a husband and wife struggling with a difficult divorce, children would be much less interested (even if they have been exposed to divorce, they have experienced it as a child of divorce, not as an adult partner).

If you decide to tell the story through the eyes of a non-child character, find a way to give that character childlike qualities or the kind of emotions or problems that a small child will easily relate to. Your POV character is the easiest way to build a bridge between your young listener and your book—don't miss this opportunity to invite a child inside your story!

--Lisa Bullard

QUESTION 8: IS IT TOO QUIET?

Maybe you think what with bedtime being the number one time that parents read to kids, publishers are clamoring for quiet books.

Not. True.

In fact, editors will often specify that they are not interested in quiet books. What is a quiet picture book? It is one where mood and setting outweigh storyline. Here are some common characteristics:

*   Mood is the most important feature.
*   The character doesn't transform.
*   There's no conflict.
*   It feels like a vignette without lasting significance for the character's life.

You probably know some classic picture books that embody some of those characteristics, like Jane Yolen's beautiful **Owl Moon** (still in print after 25 years—wow.)

And you will hear parents and teachers say they like quiet books.

And publishers do still publish quiet books. There's even Deborah Underwood's **The Quiet Book**, which explores many quiet moments a kid might experience.

But the bottom line is that the market isn't big enough. As with other small market niches (think poetry), there are indeed readers for these books. But enough readers to offset the $100,000+ production cost of a picture book? Usually not. And when publishers do put out quiet picture books, they often go with a well-known author or illustrator to tap into an existing audience for a hard-sell book. It's extremely difficult for a new author to sell a quiet book.

So, what do you do if you've written a quiet book?

First, know that a quiet book is not necessarily a bad book. Some are beautifully written, lyrical, and emotionally intense. Others just make the reader say, "So what?"

If you have gotten "too quiet" feedback, try to discern whether it is too quiet to be interesting, or too quiet to sell. Those are entirely different things. At in-person critiques, ask! If you're studying rejection letters, see if editors are just calling it too quiet, or if they're saying they love the manuscript and regret that there's no market for quiet books.

If your manuscript is too quiet to be interesting, you have failed to build tension. What does your character want, more than anything in the world? And why can't he get/have it? Restructure and rewrite your story so that your main character struggles to get what he needs and eventually succeeds.

If your manuscript is lovely but just too quiet to sell, you have lots of options.

• Try rewriting the story with more action, tension, and conflict.

• Tuck the manuscript away to try again once you are more established.

• Continue researching the market and specific editors who might be a good match for a quiet book, and continue sending your piece out, even though it's a long shot.

• Share the piece on a blog to showcase your writing.

• Submit to children's literary magazines, which might have more tolerance for quiet pieces than book publishers do.

• Chalk it up to a learning experience and vow not to write any more quiet manuscripts.

•   Vow to continue writing quiet pieces when they call to you, even knowing they are not very marketable.

•   If you're a marketing genius and you've received wonderful feedback on your manuscript from several industry professionals, you can consider self-publishing. That can be a long, difficult, expensive journey, and we don't generally recommend it for picture books. But it is an option.

As I said, lots of choices.

Writing a quiet picture book is a bit like creating a beautiful front yard garden. Lots of people might admire it as they walk by, but few people want to pay $17 to spend 10 minutes in it. So it's up to you to decide who you're creating for, what you hope to get out of the process, and what the best way is to achieve your goals.

--Laura Purdie Salas

Picture Books the Write Way

QUESTION 9: ARE THERE ILLUSTRATION ISSUES?

One of the most surprising (and often difficult) things for new picture book writers to grasp is that in most scenarios, they'll have very little direct say about the artwork. Your writing should INSPIRE amazing art possibilities, but that's where your job often ends. The usual process is that publishers maintain a "firewall" between writers and artists so that the illustrator's creative process is unhampered. They want the illustrator left free to interpret the text without feeling dictated to or trying to live up to the author's vision.

David LaRochelle, who is both a published picture book writer and illustrator, captured it perfectly when he was a guest lecturer at one of my classes: he said that it's not the writer's job to create "a paint-by-number for the illustrator."

So what does that mean for a writer? First of all, most editors DON'T want art notes included in the manuscript. Include them only when absolutely necessary (or in the few cases where a publisher asks for them). Include them only when there is an illustration detail that can't possibly be intuited from the text; this is rarely more than once or twice in a manuscript. Remember that editors (and later in the process, illustrators) are trained professionals—including overly obvious art notes will imply that you think they don't know how to do their jobs. And it can quickly label you an amateur.

If you find yourself insisting that your text needs numerous art notes, that's likely a signal that your manuscript isn't ready to submit. Go back and consider if you've included enough action and conflict (as opposed to description) to allow readers to visualize the story for themselves.

Some writers don't overuse art notes, but instead include too many unnecessary visual details in the text itself. Remember that the art should tell at least half of the story in a strong picture book. If it matters that the character has red hair, then include that detail. But if hair color is incidental, let the illustrator choose. She may even surprise you and turn your ginger-haired little girl into a black-and-white panda bear.

You may argue: but I didn't picture this as a story about pandas! Trust me on this: that's okay. That's actually great! The fact that the illustrator could take your story and make it her own is a fantastic sign. I've seen how much talented illustrators can add to my stories, things that I didn't anticipate and wouldn't have thought to ask for. If I had been able to tell them how the art SHOULD look, would those wonderful unexpected details ever have happened? Probably not.

Cutting out unnecessary visual details will also help you cut your word count, critical in today's picture book market. And if you feel strongly that you need to include description in a section of your text, then challenge yourself to create some non-visual details. Sound details are wonderful in read-aloud picture books. And it's much harder for an illustrator to capture a smell or a taste, but including a smell detail may make your writing "fresh" (excuse the pun).

You will do your best work as a writer by creating a text that allows each reader to "see" your story in his own unique way.

--Lisa Bullard

QUESTION 10: IS YOUR METER IMPERFECT?

At Mentors for Rent, we critique lots of rhyming picture books. And about 95% just don't work yet. One major reason is flawed meter. Meter is tricky, and it's something even experienced writers might struggle with.

Meter is the rhythm of your lines of verse. Let's look at the opening to my rhyming picture book, **A Leaf Can Be...**. Read out loud:

> *A leaf is a leaf.*
> *It bursts out each spring,*
> *when sunny days linger*
> *and orioles sing.*

Can you hear the beat? The flow?

The pattern of stressed (said with more emphasis) and unstressed (said with less or no emphasis) words and syllables is what creates the meter of your picture book. Here is that opening again, this time with the stressed syllables in all caps:

> a LEAF is a LEAF.
> It BURSTS out each SPRING,
> when SUNny days LINger
> and ORioles SING.

Look at a few things here. First, there are two stressed syllables in every line. Next, the second syllable of each line is also the first stressed syllable of that line. Third, there are two unstressed syllables between the first and second stressed syllables of each line. That consistency is what gives verse a pleasing, easy-to-read meter.

But different people read the same lines differently. When we are working on a rhyming manuscript with a specific meter, we can read almost any line with that meter—even if it doesn't naturally come out that way. For instance, read this:

> A leaf is a leaf.
> It bursts out each spring,
> when sunny days linger
> and orioles sing.
> One day in a bird's nest,
> I found a gold ring.

Those are NOT the next two lines in the book, thank goodness! But I bet you made them fit the meter of the first four lines. Did you read them like this?

> a LEAF is a LEAF.
> it BURSTS out each SPRING,
> when SUNny days LINger
> and ORioles SING.
> one DAY in a BIRD'S nest,
> i FOUND a gold RING.

If you did, you probably read really well out loud! However, that can hamper your own writing. Because you can make text fit an established meter, you aren't really creating lines that naturally fit the meter. If you just read those last two lines as a normal sentence, without the first four lines, where would the stresses lie?

ONE day in a BIRD'S nest, I found a GOLD RING.

Actually, that's not 100% true, because people can't all agree. Different people (or even the same people on different days!) will read these lines with different emphases. But if you came across this sentence randomly, you likely wouldn't read it like this:

one DAY in a BIRD'S nest, i FOUND a gold RING.

And that's the struggle of rhyming picture books. So, what can you do?

One option is to ditch the rhyme! Try writing your book in prose. In most cases, there's really no reason a picture book needs to be told in rhyme. Switching to prose gives you the freedom you might need to write a stronger, more appealing story.

But if you're committed to improving your meter, scan your rhyming picture book manuscript—find the meter that actually, naturally exists, not the meter you want to put into the words. My adaptation of my favorite directions (which are no longer where I originally found them) are on my website at laurasalas.com/scanning-your-poems. Try my step-by step instructions and see if they help. Know that scanning will get easier with time—I promise! Here are some other great resources:

- Lane Fredrickson's Rhyme Weaver website: http://rhymeweaver.com/

- Interactive scanning tool at For Better or Verse, from the University of Virginia: http://prosody.lib.virginia.edu/

- "Have You Got Rhythm?" by Jan Fields at the ICL site:

http://www.institutechildrenslit.com/rx/ws06/rhythm.shtml

- "Rhymer's Workshop" (a chat transcript) with Shelly Becker at the ICL site: http://www.institutechildrenslit.com/rx/tr01/sbecker.shtml

- Examples of good rhyming books on my Pinterest Boards:

  o Rhyming Nonfiction Picture Books: http://www.pinterest.com/salaslp/rhyming-nonfiction-picture-books/

  o Rhyming Picture Books: http://www.pinterest.com/salaslp/rhyming-picture-books/

Immerse yourself in learning about meter and reading excellent rhyming picture books. Then return to your manuscript. Re-read, re-feel, re-write!

Finally, find new readers. Whenever I take a rhyming manuscript to my critique group for the first time, I have someone else read it aloud. Hearing where someone else pauses or stumbles points out all my meter flaws. Even better, ask kids to read it. If five 10-year-old kids can read your rhyming picture book aloud without tripping, you've written a picture book with great meter.

--Laura Purdie Salas

REVISION CHECKLIST

_____ Does your manuscript have 13+ distinct illustration possibilities?

_____ Is it fewer than 800 words?

_____ Have you checked Amazon to determine the freshness of your premise?

_____ Have you have read many current picture books—enough to know that editors haven't already seen this storyline done this same way numerous times?

_____ Can you summarize your story problem in one short sentence?

_____ Complete this sentence: My main character wants _____, but _____. Do you have a complete story problem, with both a wish/desire and obstacles that stand in your character's way?

_____ Does your story feel like more than just a slice-of-life out of a child's day?

_____ Is the story problem one a 4-year-old can relate to?

_____ Does the ending of your story relate back to the beginning?

_____ Does your main character change somehow during the story?

_____ Does a child or childlike character solve the story problem?

_____ Is the narrator/main character a child? If not, is the narrator/main character a childlike adult or a childlike animal? If your narrator/main character is an inanimate object, have you created a character a child will really care about?

_____ Does your main character think in ways that a 4-year-old will connect with?

_____ Does the narrator/main character experience emotions that a 4-year-old will relate to?

_____ Have you avoided illustration notes—or used only one or two minimal ones?

_____ Have you left out most visual details so that the illustrator has room to create them?

_____ Is your story set in contemporary times (unless it is specifically an historical fiction picture book)?

_____ Have you used other sensory details (the way things sound or feel or smell) to create a great setting?

_____ Have you listened to at least three adults and three kids (who have never read your story) read your manuscript aloud?

_____ Did you mark where they stumbled over words and have you fixed those areas?

If your manuscript rhymes:

_____ Have you tried writing your story in prose to see if that works better?

_____ Have you scanned the meter of your manuscript?

TELL US HOW IT GOES FOR YOU!

There you have it—10 key ways to write a stronger picture book. By applying what you've read in this guide, you'll be creating a more marketable manuscript. We hope you're pleased with the results!

We love hearing progress reports and good news from our Mentors for Rent clients, and we'd love to hear from you, too. Of course we're hoping to learn that this guide was helpful, but we also want to know your suggestions for how we could make it even more useful. You can find our contact information online at MentorsForRent.com.

While you're visiting our website, we hope you'll take some time to look around. Perhaps after you use this guide to take care of some obvious issues in your picture book manuscript, you'll be interested in a picture book critique. We can also guide you through the all-important research phase, helping you identify which editors and agents might be most interested in the kind of picture book you've written. In addition to coaching/critiquing, we offer other e-books for writers: you can check them out at http://tinyurl.com/oaru3xs.

We'd be delighted to have you decide that a couple of hardworking Mentors are just what you need in your writing life!

Mentors for Rent

Three heads are better than one!

MentorsForRent.com

Laura Purdie Salas

Laura Purdie Salas has written more than 100 books for kids and teens, including ***Water Can Be...***, ***A Leaf Can Be...*** (Millbrook Press, 2012 – Minnesota Book Award Finalist, NCTE Notable, IRA Teachers' Choices, Riverby Award), and ***BookSpeak: Poems About Books*** (Clarion, 2011 – Minnesota Book Award, NCTE Notable, Bank Street Best Books, and more).

Laura started out writing and editing for adults, but a stint as an 8th-grade English teacher re-ignited her love for children's literature. She began focusing on writing for kids and never looked back.

She writes poetry, realistic fiction, and nonfiction books and articles. Laura is a member of the Children's Literature Network and SCBWI. She teaches writing for children through the Loft Literary Center in Minneapolis and is a former instructor for the Institute of Children's Literature. She loves to work with young writers through school visits and young authors conferences.

Laura's areas of expertise include poetry, nonfiction, the educational market, picture books, researching publishers, and Q&A about writing careers/the writing life. You can learn more at Laura's website and Laura's blog at laurasalas.com (just click My Blog to get to the blog). She is also on Facebook (facebook.com/LauraPSalas) and Twitter (@LauraPSalas).

Lisa Bullard

Lisa Bullard is the author of the how-to guide ***Get Started in Writing for Children*** (McGraw-Hill, 2014) and more than 80 books for young readers. Her middle grade mystery, ***Turn Left at the Cow***, was published by Harcourt in fall 2013 and will come out in paperback in spring 2015. Her picture book ***Trick-or-Treat on Milton Street*** won an International Reading Association/Children's Book Council "Children's Choice Award," a National Parenting Publications "Children's Resources Silver Award," and was named an honor title for the "Storytelling World Award." She has also won a "Teacher's Choice Award" and has been listed on the *Science Books & Films* "Best Books" list for some of her nonfiction titles for young readers. Her picture book ***You Can Write a Story! A Story-Writing Recipe for Kids*** has been a big hit with kids and teachers.

Lisa has taught children's book writing at the Loft Literary Center in Minneapolis and other locations for over 15 years. Her background includes 16 years' experience as a publishing professional; she worked for nationally renowned publishers Graywolf Press, Coffee House Press, New Rivers Press, and Lerner Publications. Lisa is a past president of the Minnesota Book Publishers Roundtable and is a graduate of the University of Denver Publishing Institute.

Lisa enjoys working with writers at all stages of development and loves to share her enthusiasm for children's books. You can learn more about Lisa by visiting lisabullard.com or by liking her author Facebook page at facebook.com/LisaBullardAuthor.

75147237R00024

Made in the USA
Lexington, KY
17 December 2017